Remember to annotate as you read.

Cinderella's Very Bad Day

by Gare Thompson

June 20, 1549, Late Morning

1   My stepsisters have been meaner than a mule today! I woke when the rooster crowed and lit a fire in the downstairs hearth, as usual. Soot and ashes from the fire covered me, as usual.

2   Next, I ran to add kindling to the fires in their rooms. I would not have heard the end of it if my stepsisters' large, ugly feet touched a cold floor. There was no kindling in either room, so I had to run to the backyard to gather up twigs and sticks. Thorns cut my fingers and briars stuck in my hair.

3   My older stepsister demanded soft-boiled eggs. My younger stepsister yelled for medium-boiled eggs. I flew to the kitchen to make their breakfasts. I toil around the clock.

Comparing
Points of View

Comparing Points of View

Student Objectives

I will be able to:

- Read, analyze, and compare the point of view of characters in related literary texts.

- Share ideas with my peers.

- Build my vocabulary knowledge.

- Write informational, narrative, and opinion texts.

Credits
Editor: Jeffrey B. Fuerst
Contributing Editors: Brett Kelly, Joanne Tangorra
Creative Director: Laurie Berger
Art Directors: Melody DeJesus, Kathryn DelVecchio-Kempa, Doug McGredy, Chris Moroch
Production: Kosta Triantafillis
Director of Photography: Doug Schneider
Photo Assistant: Jackie Friedman

Photo credits: Table of Contents B, Page 14, Back Cover: Jack climbs the bean stalk, English School, (19th century) / Private Collection / © Look and Learn / Bridgeman Images; Page 2, 12: Jack sells a cow for some beans, English School, (19th century) / Private Collection / © Look and Learn / Bridgeman Images; Page 3: The Granger Collection, NYC; Page 13: The bean stalk grows out of sight in a night, English School, (19th century) / Private Collection / © Look and Learn / Bridgeman Images; Page 15: Jack takes the talking harp, English School, (19th century) / Private Collection / © Look and Learn / Bridgeman Images; Page 17: The hen that lays golden eggs, English School, (19th century) / Private Collection / © Look and Learn / Bridgeman Images; Page 19: The giant breaks his neck, English School, (19th century) / Private Collection / © Look and Learn / Bridgeman Images

Illustrations: Lisa Manuzak: Pages 6–9; Juanbjuan Oliver: Pages 22–29

Printed in Dongguan, China. 8557/1216/12214

ISBN: 978-1-4900-9192-1

Tips for Text Annotation

As you read closely for different purposes, remember to annotate the text. Use the symbols below. Add new symbols in the spaces provided.

Symbol	Purpose
<u>underline</u>	Identify a key detail.
☆	Star an important idea in the margin.
① ② ③	Mark a sequence of events.
(magma)	Circle a key word or phrase.
?	Mark a question you have about information in the text. Write your question in the margin.
!	Indicate an idea in the text you find interesting. Comment on this idea in the margin.

Your annotations might look like this.

Notes		
	2	Next, I ran to add kindling to the fires in their rooms. I would not have heard the end
I like the way Cinderella expresses herself.		of it if my stepsisters' large, ugly feet touched a cold floor. There was no kindling in either ② room, so I had to run to the backyard to ③ gather up twigs and sticks. Thorns cut my ☆ fingers and briars stuck in my hair.
I wonder why Cinderella puts up with her mean stepsisters?	3	? My older stepsister demanded soft-boiled eggs. My younger stepsister yelled for medium-boiled eggs. I flew to the kitchen to make their breakfasts. I (toil) round the clock.

LEXILE® is a trademark of MetaMetrics, Inc., and is registered in the United States and abroad.

E-book and digital teacher's guide available at benchmarkuniverse.com.

BENCHMARK EDUCATION COMPANY
145 Huguenot Street • New Rochelle, NY • 10801

Toll-Free 1-877-236-2465
www.benchmarkeducation.com
www.benchmarkuniverse.com

Table of Contents

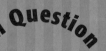

What makes people view the same experience in different ways?

4   I swept the kitchen while the eggs boiled. But dust blanketed everything, so I had to wash every dish . . . again. The eggs ended up hard-boiled.

5   "I can't eat these eggs!" they screamed. "Porridge with berries instead."

6   While picking strawberries, I forgot that they give me a rash. I was soon covered with red blotches. Still, I served the porridge. "Too hot!" cried the older stepsister. "Too cold!" shrieked the younger one. Neither wanted strawberries, so, naturally, they threw them at me. More red blotches.

STRAWBERRIES

7   Meanwhile, dear diary, my stepmother keeps screaming for me. This horrible day will never end.

Cinderella, Too Much for Words

by Gare Thompson

Characters in order of appearance

Stepsister #1
(Cinderella's Older Stepsister)

Stepmother

Stepsister #2
(Cinderella's Younger Stepsister)

Setting

Two bedrooms in the tower of a palace in a forest, an early morning in June, 1549.

Scene 1: Stepsister #1's Bedroom

Stepsister #1: *(in a loud, nasally voice)* Mother, Mother, MOTHER! Come here this instant!

Stepmother: *(racing in)* Child, what is it?

Stepsister #1: It's Cinderella. My room is freezing. What if my bare feet touch the cold floor? You know how delicate I am. I don't know what to do. I DON'T, DON'T, DON'T!

Stepmother: *(sighing)* Firstly, my dear, please do not use contractions. We are rich and can afford to use two words instead of one.

Stepsister #1: Yes, Mother, I wo—will not.

Stepmother: Good. I should have known it is Cinderella. She is horrid. She is wretched. Why, I am running out of words to describe her.

Stepsister #1: (*brightening at the chance to insult Cinderella*) Try *lazy, mean, awful, horrible, lazy…*

Stepmother: Very good! But there is no need to repeat *lazy*. Ladies of our standing—even when we are sitting—do not repeat words.

Stepsister #1: (*angrily*) Fine! But you see how bad and, um, terrible she is. (*gladly*) I will have to stay in bed all morning and not go to school.

Stepmother: I shall tell Cinderella to light your fire at once. There, there, my sweet, it will get better.

Stepsister #1: And that's—I mean, that is—not all. She put strawberries on my porridge.

Stepmother: Horrendous! Cinderella knows strawberries are your *fourth* favorite fruit! Try to rest now. I hear your sister screaming. I mean, calling.

Scene 2: Stepsister #2's Bedroom

Stepsister #2: *(shrieking)* MOTHER! I need you right this instant. NOW!

Stepmother: *(running in)* What disaster has befallen you, my child?

Stepsister #2: The disaster that has befallen me is Cinderella. She is vile. She is inhumane. She is detestable. She is . . .

Stepmother: *(smiling)* Good word choices. You might want to share some of your vocabulary with your sister. Now, what has Cinderella done to you?

Stepsister #2: Well, first she was very late, tardy one might say, and so my room was very cold, freezing one might say, when I woke up.

Stepmother: We must train her to do a better job of serving us.

Stepsister #2: *(smiling evilly)* Yes, we must. Now, what do you suppose she put on my porridge?

Stepmother: Your least favorite fruit: blueberries?

Stepsister #2: No, it was strawberries, my *most* favorite! But I saw right through her trick. So I threw the strawberries right at her as if they *were* blueberries.

Stepmother: Well, hopefully the porridge was warm and delectable.

Stepsister #2: It was not! It was colder than a snowball wrapped in an icicle.

Stepmother: Another black mark against Cinderella!

Stepsister #2: She is a thorn in our sides and a cross we have to bear.

Stepmother: Well, settle down under your covers. Rest and compose yourself, as we have to prepare for tonight's ball.

Stepsister #2: I will rest, Mother. I hope to dance with the prince all night. Cinderella is not going, is she?

Stepmother: Of course she is not going. Who would want to dance with *her*?

Notes

Folktale

Cap o' Rushes

1   Once upon a time, a rich man sent away his daughter. "You don't love me, Katie!" he said.

2   "But I love you as fresh meat loves salt," she replied. Katie was sad until she found some rushes along a river. She turned them into a cloak to cover her pretty red dress.

3   Katie was a fine lady but took a servant's job. She peeled potatoes and scrubbed pans. The other servants called her Cap o' Rushes because of her odd-looking cloak.

4   One night, Katie went to a dance wearing her red dress. Her master's son, Michael, saw her and fell in love. They danced together all evening. At midnight, she slipped off.

5   Michael looked everywhere for Katie but couldn't find her. At the next dance, when the music began to play, she reappeared. They danced together. This time, Michael followed Katie home. He saw her in the kitchen putting on her work apron. She was still beautiful. He begged Katie to marry him, and she agreed.

6   Katie's father went to the wedding. He didn't know the bride was his daughter. Katie had asked the cook to serve meat without salt. It tasted so bad that Katie's father realized he had been wrong about Katie. His daughter really did love him. They hugged each other and everyone lived happily ever after.

BuildReflectWrite

Build Knowledge

Think about how the characters are described—from another character's point of view. Then consider how they would respond to each other in a different scenario.

How does Cinderella describe her stepsisters?	How do the stepsisters describe Cinderella?

What do you think would happen if Cinderella had served the stepsisters their porridge at just the right temperature? Why?

Reflect

What makes people view the same experience in different ways?

Based on this week's texts, write down new ideas and questions you have about the essential question.

_____

_____

_____

_____

_____

_____

Writing to Sources

Informative/Explanatory

After reading the diary entry "Cinderella's Very Bad Day" and the short play "Cinderella, Too Much for Words," write an essay in which you compare and contrast your point of view on the story events to the stepsisters' points of view. Support your discussion with evidence from each text.

Notes

Jack and the Beanstalk

by the Brothers Grimm

Once upon a time, there lived a poor widow who had an only son named Jack. Times were hard. Most of their furniture had been sold to buy bread. Now they had only their cow to sell. She gave milk every morning, but one sad day the cow gave no milk.

1   "We must sell the cow. Trust me to make a good bargain," Jack said.

2   On his way to market, Jack met a butcher. The butcher was a friendly type and asked Jack what his business was. Jack told him that he was off to sell their cow. The butcher smiled and said he would make a great bargain with Jack.

3   The butcher quickly pulled out five curious-looking beans. He told a curious Jack that the beans were the most wondrous beans in the whole world.

4 He said, "If you plant them overnight, by the next morning they'll grow up and reach the sky. I will trade them for that cow of yours."

Jack sells the cow for magic beans

5 "Done!" cried Jack, who was so delighted with the bargain that he ran all the way home to tell his mother how lucky he had been.

6 His mother, however, was very disappointed and so angry she threw the beans out of the window into the garden and sent poor Jack to bed without any supper.

7 When he woke up the next morning, the room was almost dark. Running to the window, Jack saw the sun was shining brightly, but beside his window there was a giant beanstalk that stretched up and up as far as he could see, into the sky. He went outside to get a better look.

② Jack climbs the beanstock and finds the giants castle

8   "I'll just see where it leads to," thought Jack, so he stepped out of the window onto the beanstalk and climbed up and up. Finally reaching the top, Jack found himself in a new and beautiful country. He saw a great castle, with a broad road leading to the front gate.

9   As Jack drew near to the huge castle, he saw a giant's wife standing at the door.

10   "If you please, ma'am," said he, "would you kindly give me some breakfast? I have had nothing to eat since yesterday."

11   Now, the giant's wife, although very big and very ugly, had a kind heart. So she said: "Very well, little man, come in. You must be quick about it, for if my husband, the giant, finds you here, he will eat you up, bones and all."

Notes

12   The giant's wife gave him a good breakfast, but before Jack had half-finished it there came a terrible knock at the front door. It seemed to shake even the thick walls of the castle.

13   "That is my husband!" said the giantess, in a terrible fright. "We must hide you." She lifted Jack up and popped him into the empty kettle.

14   No sooner had the giant's wife opened the door than her husband roared out:

15   "Fee, fi, fo, fum,
I smell the blood of an Englishman;
Be he alive, or be he dead, I'll grind his bones to make my bread!"

16   "Where is the boy?" he continued. "I'll have him for my breakfast."

17   "Nonsense!" said his wife. "It's the ox I am making for your dinner that you smell."

18   So the giant sat down and ate the whole ox. When he had finished, he said: "Wife, bring me my money bags." So his wife brought him two full bags of gold, and the giant began to count his money. But he was so sleepy that his head began to nod. Then he began to snore, like the rumbling of thunder.

19   Jack crept out of his hiding spot and snatched up the two bags. The giant's dog barked loudly, but Jack made his way down the beanstalk before the giant awoke.

20   Jack and his mother were now quite rich. But Jack wanted to visit the giant's castle again. So while his mother was away at market, Jack climbed up, and up, and up, until he was at the top again.

21   The giantess was standing at the door. However, she did not recognize Jack, as he was dressed in fine clothes. "If you please, ma'am," said he, "will you give me some breakfast?"

22   "Run away," said she. "My husband the giant will eat you up, bones and all. The last boy who came here stole two bags of gold. So off with you!" Yet the giantess kindly allowed Jack to come into the kitchen, and set before him a giant breakfast. Soon there was a great rumbling like an earthquake. The giantess had only time to bundle Jack into the oven when in came the giant.

23   Once inside, the giant roared:

24   "Fee, fi, fo, fum,
I smell the blood of an Englishman;
Be he alive, or be he dead,
I'll grind his bones to make my bread!"

25   But his wife told him he was mistaken. The giant ate and then called out: "Wife, bring the little brown hen!" The giantess went out and brought in a little brown hen. She placed the hen on the table.

26   "Lay!" said the giant; and the hen at once laid a golden egg. He commanded the hen to lay three more golden eggs. It did.

27   "That will do for today," said the giant, and he went to sleep. Once he was snoring, Jack snatched up the hen and ran. The hen cackled, and the giant woke up. But before he moved, Jack had escaped and was home safely.

28   The little brown hen and the golden eggs made Jack and his mother richer than ever. Still, Jack was always thinking about the beanstalk. One day he crept out of the window again, and climbed up, and up, and up, and up, until he reached the top.

29   This time Jack crept round to the back of the castle. When the giant's wife went out for a moment, he slipped into the kitchen and hid in the oven.

30   In came the giant, roaring louder than ever:

31   "Fee, fi, fo, fum,
I smell the blood of an Englishman;
Be he alive, or be he dead,
I'll grind his bones to make my bread!"

32   But the giantess said she had seen no boys. So the giant sat down to breakfast. When he had finished eating, he called out: "Wife, bring me the golden harp!" So she brought in the golden harp. "Sing!" said the giant. The harp sang the most beautiful songs. It sang the giant asleep.

33   Jack seized the golden harp, but the harp called out. The giant woke up and saw Jack running out. He dashed after Jack. Holding the harp tightly, Jack ran as fast as he could.

34   The giant chased, close behind. Jack climbed down the beanstalk. So did the giant. Jack called out: "Mother, bring me an axe!" His mother did. Upon reaching the ground, Jack cut the beanstalk in two. Down came the giant with a terrible crash! And that was the end of him. No one knows what happened to the giantess, but Jack and his mother lived happily ever after.

The Giant's Complaint

1   Hello, officer. I'm the giant and I'm here to complain about how the fairy tales always make me out to be a bad guy. What did I do that was so terrible? Is it my fault that I'm so huge, and that my voice booms like a kettledrum?

2   Did I ever blow your house down? No! Gobble up your sweet old grandma? No! I'm not a wolf! In fact, I'm as gentle as a lamb.

3   That tale about Jack and his beanstalk is a bunch of hooey. The true story is that we were nice to the little guy. My wife fed him and treated him as a guest. But instead of being grateful, Jack stole a bag of gold from us. I was so mad that my face turned purple. I wanted to use his bones to grind my bread!

4   If someone stole your gold, wouldn't you try to catch him? Of course you would. You wouldn't waste a single moment. You would chase after him as fast as your legs—or bicycle, or what-have-you—could carry you.

5   But unfortunately, I wasn't able to catch Jack. So he returned and then stole my favorite hen, and next my beautiful golden harp.

6   Even worse, at the end of the story, Jack is the one who lives happily ever after, not me. Well, I'm fed up! That's why I'm here to complain to the fairy-tale and fable police. Do I need to fill out a form?

Notes

BuildReflectWrite

Build Knowledge

Determine the authors' purpose for including the following characters. Describe how these characters move the plot forward.

Butcher	Giant's Wife	Brown Hen

Reflect

What makes people view the same experience in different ways?

Based on this week's texts, write down new ideas and questions you have about the essential question.

_____

_____

_____

_____

_____

_____

Writing to Sources

Narrative

Now that you have read "Cinderella, Too Much for Words" and "Jack and the Beanstalk," imagine what would happen if Cinderella's stepmother met Jack's mother. Using details from these two stories, write a short play in which Jack's mother and Cinderella's stepmother talk about their children. Make sure you choose a title for your play.

The True Jack?

by Gare Thompson

Cast of Characters

Host

Mom
(*Jack's Mother*)

Cow

Giantess

Butcher

Giant

Setting

A castle in the late 1600s.

(A small group of lords, ladies, craftsmen, and peasants sit on benches, the floor, and other places in the room; they are the audience for what is essentially a seventeenth-century talk show. The Host sits across a table, interviewing Cow.)

Host: Welcome, all! Thanks for coming to *Inside Fairy Tales*. Today we're meeting with many of the people who know Jack, from "Jack and the Beanstalk" fame. What is he really like? My first guest is the cow. So, from your point of view, what is Jack like?

Cow: *(in a hurt voice)* Well, first of all, my name is Sam. Jack never called me by my name. It was always about Jack.

Host: Are you saying Jack was selfish?

Cow: Do cows moo? The boy is young, so maybe he'll change. But he got rid of me just like that. A couple of dry days and—Bingo!—traded.

Host: That doesn't sound very nice, but I believe Jack did need to trade you. He didn't have a choice.

Cow: *(angry)* Oh, that's what they all say.

Host: All?

Cow: All the fairy-tale heroes are the same. They just want to be rich. Or famous. Or both. They are all selfish, including Jack. Especially Jack.

Host: What else could Jack have done?

Cow: If he needed money, he could have found a job on another farm. Jack is a selfish young man. That's my point of view about Jack.

Host: Well, there you have it. Sam the Cow says Jack is a selfish young man. Now let's see what the butcher has to say. Mr. Butcher, thanks for joining us. Tell us your point of view of Jack.

Butcher: *(jolly)* Bless my stars, he was a kind lad. Yes, he seemed kind to me.

(Cow shakes her head in disagreement.)

Host: You think he was kind. Why?

Butcher: The boy just wanted to make sure his mother had food and clothes. *(pauses)* And smart! He knew a good deal. Look how the beans changed his life. I'm sure he's going to give a lot of his money to people who need it.

Cow: He hasn't given me a thing! Selfish!

Host: It seems that others don't believe Jack is so kind. What else makes you think he is kind?

Butcher: Jack had tears in his eyes when he handed over the cow. His hands were shaking. You could tell he didn't want to trade the cow. He had no choice.

Cow: Horsefeathers!

Host: What are your final words on Jack?

Butcher: He was a kind and smart boy. *(smiles)* I have some seeds with me. Want to trade that nice diamond ring?

Host: *(turns his ring)* No thanks, Butcher. *(to audience)* Well, folks, there you have it. The butcher claims Jack is kind and smart. Now let's see what Jack's mother has to say. Mothers often have a special point of view. *(to Mom)* Mom—may I call you Mom?—tell us all what Jack was like as a child.

Mom: Oh, he was a sweet, happy child. *(pauses)* But he could never sit still. A regular jumping bean. I had to watch him like a hawk. He would run about and leap off trees without a thought.

Host: Jack was a daredevil from early on.

Mom: Yes, he was! He often would act first, and think later.

Host: So—Jack was impulsive?

Mom: Oh my, yes. Many's the time I wished I had a leash for him. I had to keep an eye on him 24/7.

Host: Was Jack a good worker?

Mom: Well, he wasn't lazy. . . . Decision-making was not Jack's strong suit. He'd lose focus easily. He'd be milking the cow and then he'd see a butterfly and chase it. The milk would go sour.

Host: Now, Mom, I understand you were upset when Jack came home with those beans.

Mom: I was tied to a fit. I mean fit to be tied. What a foolish boy. I was sure the butcher had taken advantage of Jack.

Butcher: (*shouting*) It was a fair trade.

Cow: (*shouting*) I told you he should never have traded me. Silly *and* selfish.

Host: Quiet back there. (*to audience*) It seems we have some different opinions about Jack and what happened.

Mom: Well, it turned out right in the end. But I hope he doesn't keep making—what was that word? Oh yes: *impulsive* decisions.

Host: Let's sum up your point of view. Jack is impulsive and acts before he thinks.

Mom: Yes, but he's a good boy.

Host: There you have it! Three guests, three different points of view. Let's see what some other characters from "Beanstalk" thought of Jack. First, we'll talk with the giantess.

Host: Giantess, you were the first person to meet Jack when he climbed up the beanstalk. Is that right?

Giantess: I was outside the castle taking a break from cooking. My husband eats a lot. I was resting my eyes for a spell. When I opened them, there was Jack. He looked tired and hungry.

Host: Jack asked you for food?

Giantess: He did. Those were the first words out of his mouth. No "Hello" or "How are you?" Being kind, I asked him in.

Host: And then what happened?

Giantess: Jack sat at the table and ate. He may be little, but the boy can eat big-time. Then my husband came home.

Host: Not good timing.

Giantess: Terrible! My husband hates boys. Actually, he likes them—as a snack! I hid Jack and told my husband to chow down. Then he counted his gold, which he does every Friday like clockwork.

Host: Jack took the gold?

Giantess: *Stole* is the word! My husband fell asleep. Then, before I could say "Boo!," Jack stole the gold. He is a greedy boy.

Host: Jack came back to the castle, right?

Giantess: (*nods*) That time he stole my husband's hen.

Host: The hen that lays golden eggs.

Giantess: (*nods again*) He snuck into the castle again and stole the golden harp. Jack is the greediest boy I know.

Host: Greedy? Well, let's see what others have to say about Jack. Make room, please, for Mr. Giant.

Giant: Coming through! *Ouch!* You need to make the ceilings higher here.

Host: Now, Giant, what is your point of view about Jack?

Giant: I have a big point of view about that boy. After all, I am a giant. I have the biggest point of view.

Host: You're big and you have a big point of view. Tell us what it is, please.

Giant: I think Jack is small. He is smaller than other boys I've e't, I mean met. However, he is the biggest thief.

Mom: My son is a good boy.

Giant: He is a big thief. Jack stole my gold, my hen, and my harp.

Host: By the way, how did you get the gold, the hen, and the harp?

Mom: He stole them from Jack's father!

(Cow and Butcher gasp loudly.)

Giant: We're talking about Jack, not me. Jack is the thief.

Host: So you think Jack is a thief. What else do you have to say about him?

Giant: Jack is mean. He is meaner than an angry snake. He is the meanest lad in the land.

Host: Jack is a thief, but how is he mean?

Giant: He chopped the beanstalk down while I was on it. I'm lucky I didn't die.

Host: We all thought you did die.

Giant: You thought wrong. I got a broken leg, and the town got a hole in the ground that is now a fishpond. But I'm alive. No thanks to that mean thief, Jack.

Host: Thank you, Giant, for that point of view. *(to audience)* What is your point of view about Jack? Is he lucky? A good boy? Mean? Greedy? Is he impulsive? Kind and smart? Selfish? Or is he something else entirely? You decide.

29

Notes

Fantasy

The Beanstalk Experiment

1   Jack and his friend Rayna conducted a science experiment. Jack planted one of the beans that he found in the giant's house. Meanwhile, Rayna planted a regular green bean.

2   A week later, Jack's bean sprouted and grew two feet in one night. Rayna's bean sprouted too, but it was only one inch high.

3   After four weeks, here were the results of their experiment.

Jack and Rayna's Beanstalk Experiment				
	Week 1	Week 2	Week 3	Week 4
Jack's bean	12 feet	44 feet	1,178 feet	5,280 feet
Rayna's bean	1 inch	3 inches	8 inches	13 inches

4   Jack said his bean is the best because it grew the tallest. "In fact," he boasted to Rayna, "my beanstalk is one mile high, because 5,280 feet equals one mile. And it is so sturdy that I can climb up it high into the sky."

5   Rayna shook her head. "But Jack," she said, "all you have is a beanstalk and leaves. You don't have any beans to eat!"

6   She showed Jack the new green beans growing on her beanstalk. "Pretty soon," boasted Rayna, "my beans will be ready to eat. That's why my beanstalk is the best!"

7   You be the judge. Who has the best beanstalk? Why do you think so?